# Tour of Wharram Percy

*Above:* *The 2,000-year-old track into Wharram Percy makes a series of switch-backs to cross the valley, probably leading to the village's early name 'Warum', meaning 'at the bends'. The earthworks of the village are visible in the field beyond*

## TRACK TO THE VILLAGE

The track leading from the car park into the valley was in use in the Late Iron Age (about 50 BC) and perhaps even as early as the Late Bronze Age (about 1000 BC) as part of a network that connected numerous small farming communities. The track enters and leaves the main valley via natural side-valleys, but the prolonged footfall of people and livestock has further eroded these natural gulleys to form deep 'green lanes' or 'hollow ways'. This track, the main east–west route through the medieval village, continued in use until the late 20th century. For most of the Middle Ages, just as today, the track would have approached the village through an intensively farmed arable landscape.

In the valley bottom, a culvert built alongside the Malton and Driffield Branch Railway (closed in 1965) now carries the tiny stream always known as the Beck, which was so important to the medieval village.

## ENTRY INTO THE VILLAGE

From the valley floor, the medieval track gently ascends into the village. The valley side was once part of a long village green, at whose southern end stood the church. Peasants were entitled to graze cattle and

geese on this green and two circular livestock pounds have been identified here. The current coniferous plantation on the opposite valley side, called Nut Wood from the 1850s and simply The Holt (meaning a wood) in earlier centuries, originated as an enclosed medieval coppice. The woodland would have been an important resource, owned and carefully managed by the lords of the manor.

In 1254, Peter Percy I (d.1266 or 1267) became outright lord of Wharram Percy. It was he, perhaps, who tried to create a more regular village plan by establishing the so-called North and East Rows of peasant houses. The East Row was built on the village green and was probably home to 'cottars', or cottagers, the lowest rank of peasant tenants.

*Below:* *The track into the village, with the East Row to the left*

To maximize the size of the plots in this new row, the original track across the green was re-routed to the highest possible level on the slope, descending again to reach the church. Despite this, some of the awkwardly shaped plots on the steep, boggy slope were never occupied, leaving gaps in what was intended as a continuous frontage of dwellings.

The main track must often have been busy with pedestrians, carts and herded livestock. It is often imagined that rubbish and sewage were flung into streets from adjacent houses, but finds from the surrounding fields suggest that waste was collected for use as fertilizer.

# The structure of peasant society

The word 'peasant' (*paysan* in Norman French) referred to any country-dweller. At the lowest level of peasant society (apart from homeless beggars and outlaws), the 'cottar', or cottager, held no land other than the 'toft' (the cottage and its surrounding garden), no livestock and no plough. Cottars paid rent to the lord of the manor in the form of labour, while making extra wages when possible as hired hands. The small plots of the East Row were perhaps home to cottars.

The next rank was the 'villein' (or serf), who typically held a toft, a 'croft' (a strip of land adjoining the toft) and one or two 'oxgangs' (each of 7ha) in the open fields. He paid rent to the lord in the form of service, produce or cash. Villeins could not give up their homes or land, or marry, without their lord's permission and their children were born into the same class. The West Row (north) and North Row were home to villeins. The regularity of these plots reflected the order and stability that a good lord was expected to provide. The most prominent villeins were required to act as 'graves' (or 'reeves'), administering their lord's own land. Twelve villeins served as jurors in the manor court, hearing minor cases and meting out fines and punishments.

Free peasants, or 'sokemen', were subject to fewer ties and obligations than villeins. They appear to have had a higher status and were probably wealthier, though surviving documents tell us very little about them. Freedom from an overlord presented more opportunities, but also more risks, because the family did not benefit from the lord's protection. The West Row (south) longhouses may have been home to sokemen.

When a lord made a village his usual place of residence, he would promote outward signs of his good lordship, such as an imposing manor house, an up-to-date church, a hunting park, decent peasant housing, and well-tended woods, fields and meadows. All these are in evidence at Wharram Percy in the late 13th and early 14th centuries.

*Below: 14th-century illustration of an overseer supervising the harvest*

## WHARRAM PERCY COTTAGES AND 18TH-CENTURY FARMYARD

Wharram Percy Cottages are a row of three Victorian agricultural labourers' cottages built soon after 1845. The cottages incorporate the shell of a single-storey, two-room farm building constructed in the mid 1770s, the outline of which can still be seen in the external walls. This building formed the southern side of a farmyard built over the course of that decade. The irregularly shaped ground-plan suggests that the 1770s building may in turn have been based upon a still earlier building, perhaps dating to the 17th century. By about 1800, the cobbled farmyard was enclosed on the west by a tiled range comprising a barn, stables and granary and on the east by a thatched range which included cart sheds. These ranges were dismantled in stages from 1836 onwards and their excavated remains are displayed. The

*Above: Looking east towards the post-medieval farmyard and cottages*

**A** *18th-century farmyard*
**B** *Wharram Percy Cottages*
**C** *Station sign moved here in 1978*
**D** *Footings of the farmhouse built in 1807*

Victorian cottages were inhabited until 1976 and then used every summer until 1990 as accommodation for archaeologists.

## POST-MEDIEVAL FARMHOUSES

The visible foundations, revealed by excavations in 1985–9, are those of a fairly grand farmhouse constructed in 1807 to replace a dilapidated predecessor built shortly before 1674. This late 17th-century farmhouse was built over the vestiges of medieval peasant houses, but there was no direct continuity from the medieval village.

**Post-medieval farm and cottages**

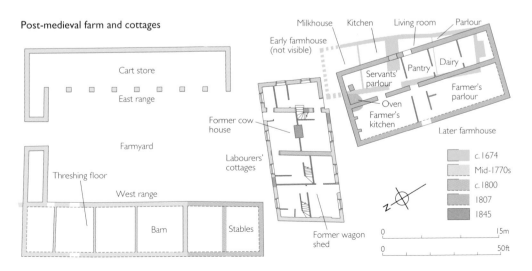

The late 17th-century farmhouse was a modest, timber-framed building, home to a sheep farmer named William Botterell and his household, tenants of the wealthy Buck family. An inventory made following his death in March 1699 describes a parlour (Botterell's parlour and bedchamber), a 'fore room' (the living and dining room) and a kitchen on the ground floor, each with a bedchamber above, plus a lean-to 'milkhouse' or dairy.

In 1806, a surveyor working for the new landlord, Lord Middleton of Birdsall, reported that 'Most of the Buildings on this Farm are in a decayed State, and very insufficient for a Farm of such Magnitude, it is necessary a New Dwelling House, and other Conveniencies, should be built'. His advice was acted upon and a new farmhouse was built the following year. An inventory of 1830 describes the rooms, outlines of which are displayed: a front parlour for the farmer (containing a bookcase, carpet, barometer and seven chairs), a back parlour for the servants (containing a bed,

*Above: This 1834 painting by Mary Ellen Best, of a kitchen from a small manor house in nearby Driffield, gives an impression of the farmhouse described in the 1830 inventory*

stove, desk and another seven chairs), a kitchen (containing a mangle, clock and six more chairs), three bedchambers (the smartest containing a mirror), a bedroom for servant girls, and a garret dormitory for eight labourers. The farmhouse was demolished soon after 1845, as landlords invested in more accessible farms on surrounding high ground.

## MEDIEVAL AND LATER VICARAGES

The vicars of Wharram Percy appear to have lived in various houses close to the North Manor until about 1327 when a new vicarage was built just to the north of the church. This had an adjoining garden and a detached barn to store grain from the two strip fields allocated to the vicar.

In 1546, the vicar Marmaduke Atkinson built two heated parlours, with three bedchambers above, in the space between the medieval house and barn, probably creating an L-shaped building under one roof. But in February or March 1553, a fire broke out in the barn and destroyed the whole building; the excavated foundations of the burnt barn are displayed. Before his departure the following year, Atkinson built a new 'hall house' immediately in front of the site of the destroyed one, with a detached kitchen, stable and hen house. The barn was not rebuilt, as the two fields allocated to the vicar had been

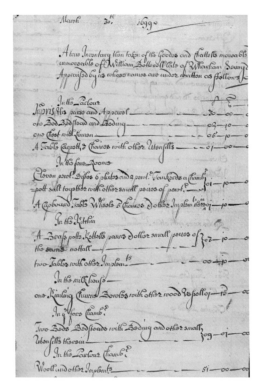

*Above: Inventory of the early farmhouse made following the death of William Botterell in 1699. Wool worth £51 – by far the most costly item on the inventory – was stored in the parlour bedchamber, providing both security from theft and insulation for Botterell's parlour directly below*

*Above:* The foundations of vicarage buildings displayed to the north of the church, viewed from the north-west

**A** Footings of 18th-century vicarage

**B** Sunken dairy of 18th-century vicarage

**C** 18th-century conduit taking fresh water to farmhouse

**D** Footings of vicarage barn of about 1327

converted to pasture in the 1540s, the village's other arable lands having been lost in 1527.

By the 1580s the house was said to be 'in great decay' and by 1604 it had been let to two farmers who had allowed it to fall further into 'ruins and decaie'. The vicar, Thomas Pearson, was ordered to make repairs and, after his death in 1618, successive vicars appear to have inhabited the house again. By 1674, however, it had been rebuilt once more, further downslope and at right angles to its predecessors. By 1716, the slope down to the stream was occupied by an orchard, which survived into the 20th century and was replanted in the wake of the excavations. Finally, in the early 18th century, another vicarage was built alongside its predecessor. It had four ground-floor rooms with four bedchambers above, and a sunken dairy to the rear (foundations of all of these are displayed). Demolished in 1835, it was later described as having been 'a mere cottage with stable adjoining, both covered in thatch'.

## ST MARTIN'S CHURCH

A church dedicated to St Martin was probably built here in the late 10th century. As it is neither on high ground, nor next to a manor house, its location puzzled researchers for many decades. Recent studies, however, have suggested that churches (as well as other buildings used by the whole community) were often built by free peasants (see feature on page 2) on the only land available to them, namely the village green. The location of St Martin's appears to fit this pattern.

### Sequence of vicarages

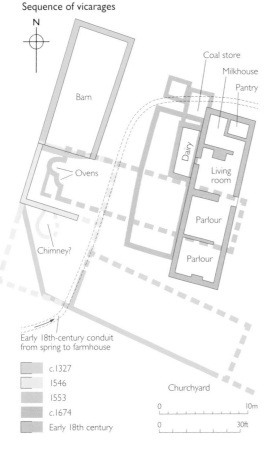

N

Coal store
Milkhouse
Pantry
Barn
Dairy
Ovens
Living room
Parlour
Chimney?
Parlour

Early 18th-century conduit from spring to farmhouse

c.1327
1546
1553
c.1674
Early 18th century

Churchyard

0   10m
0   30ft

*Above: The interior of the church looking south-east. The architecture reveals how the building has been changed over time*

**A** *Site of c.950 timber church*
**B** *Footprint of c.1050 stone church*
**C** *Blocked window of c.1125*

**D** *Arcade of c.1175 between the nave and the south aisle (demolished c.1550)*
**E** *Arch of c.1550, built using decorated stones of c.1175*

## Architectural Details

*Above: Fragments of high status grave covers dating to the 12th to 14th centuries were incorporated into the walls of the church in the mid 16th century*

*Above: Detail from a 14th-century window, one of several carved masks around the church. Some are stylized, but others reveal details of medieval hairstyles and clothing*

*Below: Reconstructions illustrating the growth and decline of the church and village at Wharram Percy*

The original 10th-century timber church was discovered through excavation as a pattern of postholes for vertical timbers. This tiny rectangular structure was overlain in the mid 11th century, a decade or two before the Norman Conquest, by the first stone church, the outline of which is now marked out with paving slabs. A distinctive set of burials, covered with reused Roman grave slabs, may represent a group of prominent free peasants responsible for this rebuilding (see page 16).

In subsequent years the church was enlarged and later reduced in size. In part this reflects the fluctuating population of the village, but sponsoring architectural improvements to the church was also a way for the village's noble families to broadcast their lordly credentials. The Percy family perhaps built the south aisle when they became the major

c.1050

c.1125

c.1175

St Martin's Church

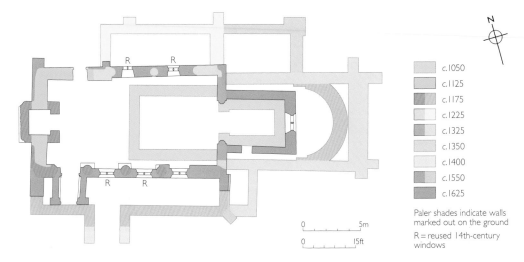

c.1050
c.1125
c.1175
c.1225
c.1325
c.1350
c.1400
c.1550
c.1625

Paler shades indicate walls marked out on the ground
R = reused 14th-century windows

0 _____ 5m

0 _____ 15ft

landlords in the village soon after 1166 and continued to enhance the building in keeping with changing architectural style and liturgical practice once they achieved outright control in 1254. Similarly, the Hiltons, who became lords of Wharram about 1400, replaced the upper storey of the bell tower and adorned it prominently with their family arms.

St Martin's served the whole parish, including the surviving village of Thixendale and three others that were all deserted by the 17th century: Burdale, Raisthorpe and Towthorpe. As a result, the church was maintained long after Wharram Percy's population had dwindled to a single household. In 1870, when a new church was built in Thixendale to save the residents of that village a 5-mile round trip, St Martin's became effectively redundant. After a final marriage ceremony took place in 1928, no further repairs were carried out and within 40 years the church was in ruins. A storm in December 1959 led to the collapse of the

*Above: The dilapidated interior of the church in 1954*

bell tower. The whole interior was excavated between 1962 and 1974, and the decision was then taken to remove the decaying roof and conserve the building as a ruin.

South of the church, the graveyard retains headstones of late 18th- and 19th-century date, some of which bear surnames still found locally. Principally for this reason, archaeological excavation was restricted to the northern side of the churchyard (see feature page 18).

c.1400

c.1550

c.1845

## MILLPOND

The availability of fresh water from the tiny stream was once thought to have been a critical factor in determining the location of the village, but the stream was probably most valued as a source of power, since watercourses on the Wolds that can be relied upon year-round are very rare. Two mills are documented within the village, but only one of these has been located, at the north end of the millpond. Excavations revealed that the earliest mill dam was built in this location in the late ninth or early tenth century, possibly by the same free peasants who built the church, to serve as a communal facility. Little of the mill itself was discovered, but it probably had a horizontal millwheel with simple gearing to turn the stones and therefore probably did not

# Everyday life for Wharram's peasants

Wharram Percy's medieval inhabitants depended almost entirely on farming. As a result, the rhythm of the seasons structured their lives. A mixed economy of livestock and crops created a cycle of successive peaks of activity through the year: hedge-laying; lambing; ploughing; sowing; shearing; hay mowing; harvesting; cheese-making; slaughtering; cloth-making. The lord's periodic demands for assistance with these same tasks must have been unwelcome intrusions.

The popular image of peasant life – of grinding poverty and unrelenting hardship – certainly holds good for the lowest levels of society, but the sizes of the standard landholdings at Wharram suggest that, certainly from the mid 14th century, most

'villein' and free families could have made a reasonable living under normal circumstances (see page 14). According to age and sex, each member of the household had their allotted tasks. For some activities, the whole family would have risen before dawn, while the most intensive operations at harvest time would also have required the employment of servants or landless 'cottars' (see page 2). The husband was responsible for much of the more physical work, although a widowed woman (until or unless she remarried) would take over all the farm labour of her husband.

A married woman looked after the house and toft, especially the garden, and was also responsible for dairying, for looking after the geese and hens, for harvesting with a sickle (men usually used scythes), for brewing ale after the harvest, and for

spinning and weaving through the winter. Fetching pails of water from the Beck and carrying dough to bake in the common oven were parts of her daily routine. Bone studies show that the women of Wharram had much more muscular arms than their counterparts in towns and that they spent many hours squatting to wash clothes by the Beck and to cook on the hearth in the open hall. Finding fuel for the fire was probably a constant chore, because the parish had so little woodland: some households burned dried cow dung, while others bought coal and peat from passing traders.

*Above: In this illustration of about 1275 a peasant using a billhook collects sticks from a coppiced tree*
*Left: A woman with a baby stirs a cooking pot on an open fire while a small child works the bellows, in this illustration of about 1320*

require a specialist miller. By the late 12th or early 13th century, the mill had been taken over by one of the lords of the manor, and probably rebuilt with a vertical wheel. The lord would probably have appointed a miller, part of whose job was to ensure that his master's tenants paid for the service.

By the 16th century, only the pond near the church survived, having been converted into a watering hole for livestock. The pond became silted and was recreated following excavations from 1972 to 1981.

## PEASANT FARMSTEADS IN THE WEST ROW (SOUTH)

On the plateau overlooking the church, the wall-lines of an excavated peasant longhouse and two adjoining barns, all dating to the 14th and 15th centuries, are displayed. Along the length of each building, large padstones would have supported timber 'crucks' – huge, curving beams, ideally of oak but sometimes of ash – arranged like the ribs of an upturned boat. The crucks were strong enough to carry a good, high, thatched roof, which allowed for interiors almost as spacious and comfortable as contemporary timber-framed town houses, like many that survive in nearby York. It has been estimated that in about 1300, 500 of these large timbers would have been in use within the village, almost all of which must have been imported, because Wharram had very little woodland of its own. This particular longhouse is far larger than most of the other peasant buildings in the village and fragments of expensive window glass were found during the excavation. Indeed, the whole layout of this part of the settlement differs from the regular pattern visible further north along the plateau (see page 11). Partly on this evidence, it has been suggested that this area was occupied by free peasants, the social group probably responsible for founding St Martin's church and rebuilding it in stone. This excavated longhouse and its neighbours therefore probably represent the homes of wealthier peasants.

At the top of the steep slope immediately above the gate from the churchyard lies the earthwork of

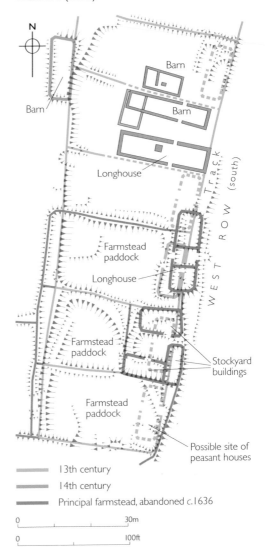

West Row (south)

N

Barn

Barn

Barn

Longhouse

Farmstead paddock

Longhouse

Farmstead paddock

Stockyard buildings

Farmstead paddock

Possible site of peasant houses

Track (south)

WEST ROW (south)

13th century

14th century

Principal farmstead, abandoned c.1636

0 _____ 30m

0 _____ 100ft

another remarkable longhouse. This building's wall-lines are so clear that they prompted one of Maurice Beresford's earliest excavations, in 1952. Like the excavated example further north along the plateau, this longhouse was fairly large and divided into three rooms whose limits can be traced, but this example is distinguished by its odd position: it encroached into the neighbouring plot and into the lane that once ran along the edge of the plateau. Many such breakdowns in the regulation of development occurred in the wake of the Great Famine of 1315–17 and the Black Death of 1349.

*Left: A reconstructed cooking pot made in nearby Staxton and found at Wharram*

Careful plotting of the earthworks shows that the house was linked to a farm complex, with a stockyard, paddocks and outbuildings. It was conceivably the last medieval building to remain occupied: the 'chief messuage', or principal farmstead, which belonged to John Richardson in 1617. Richardson lived and farmed at Wharram Percy until he moved to nearby North Grimston in about 1636, after which the house was apparently dismantled.

*Above: The South Manor undercroft was excavated in 1955. The remains of a fireplace are visible in the right-hand wall*

## SOUTH MANOR

The South Manor was probably constructed soon after 1166. It comprised a substantial house and various outbuildings, set within a large rectangular enclosure surrounded by a wall with an external ditch. The house, most of which has not been excavated, appears to have spanned the frontage of the plot so that it dominated the skyline. The undercroft of the manor house's smarter 'high end' was discovered in 1955; well-built stone walls 3m deep were found beneath the foundations of a sequence of later small peasant houses. A large open hall would probably have stood adjacent to the manor house's high end, with a pantry and buttery beyond (and probably with a detached kitchen), but none of these elements has yet been securely located or excavated. The smart, stone-vaulted undercroft, which was accessed via a ramp that may have come up within or immediately outside the open hall, was warmed by a large fireplace and may have been reserved for the lord's private business meetings. Above it, probably reached via a room at the north end of the open hall, was a 'solar', a room for the private use of the family, comfortably furnished and well lit by south-facing glazed windows. In 1254, Peter Percy I (c.1206–66) became outright lord of the manor; he seems to have demolished the South Manor and built or rebuilt the more spacious and secluded North Manor house. The stone window tracery, which could not easily be reused, was thrown back into the undercroft, but the remaining stone was taken away. Peasant houses were then built over the site.

**South Manor area**

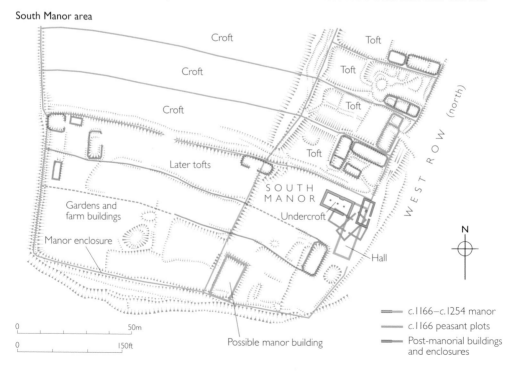

Croft

Croft

Croft

Toft

Toft

Toft

Toft

Later tofts

SOUTH MANOR

Undercroft

WEST ROW (north)

Gardens and farm buildings

Manor enclosure

Hall

N

Possible manor building

0   50m

0   150ft

━━━ *c.*1166–*c.*1254 manor
─── *c.*1166 peasant plots
━━ Post-manorial buildings and enclosures

*Above: Reconstruction looking south along the West Row (north) in about 1300, with a typical peasant longhouse cutaway*

## WEST ROW (NORTH)

Immediately to the north of the South Manor, and evidently built as part of the same planned development of about 1166, lay a row of six regular peasant plots, each 60 feet (18.3m) wide, plus one half-width plot. The occupants were 'villeins', or unfree peasants, who rented their homes and land from their lord by providing service, produce or cash. Each plot comprised a 'toft' and a 'croft', one of the most easily recognizable units of medieval planned villages.

The toft contained the 'messuage' – the house and any ancillary buildings – together with a back garden ('garth'), or sometimes just a yard where cattle were kept over winter. Each toft originally contained a single dwelling or longhouse which spanned the frontage. In time, this pattern evidently broke down, with the realignment of some longhouses and the insertion of other dwellings, barns and outbuildings within the original garth.

The longhouses at Wharram are typical of peasant houses across England, which,

*Left: An aerial photograph of the West Row (north) and South Manor site, looking north-west*

**A** *Earthwork remains of peasant longhouse (illustrated above)*
**B** *Medieval track*
**C** *Area of toft*
**D** *Area of croft*
**E** *North Manor*
**F** *South Manor*
**G** *Outline of vaulted stone undercroft of South Manor*

regardless of differing local building materials and styles, comprised three rooms arranged in the same pattern. In the middle, the 'open hall', with opposed front and back doors at one end, was the most public room, where guests were entertained and business done. A fireplace near the centre of the floor was the house's main source of artificial light and heat, and was also where most of the cooking was done. The beaten earth floor, perhaps covered with a thin scatter of scented rushes, was kept scrupulously clean. The room was open right to the roof to allow the smoke to percolate out through the thatch, in the process preserving cheeses and joints of meat hanging overhead, as well as keeping the thatch free of vermin and nesting birds. Towards the end of the Middle Ages, a smoke hood or chimney was often built, allowing an upstairs room to be inserted into the open hall. Windows (usually unglazed, but closed with shutters when necessary) lit a trestle table along **the cross-wall further from the opposing doors, wh**ere the family would eat, all facing towards the fireplace. Behind the table, a doorway led to the 'high end' of the

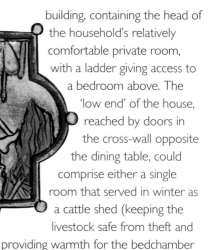

*Above:* A peasant warms his feet by an open fire in this manuscript illustration of about 1275. Preserved foodstuffs hang from a beam overhead

*Below:* Detail from a manuscript of about 1330 showing a peasant woman feeding chickens while holding a distaff and spindle for spinning yarn

building, containing the head of the household's relatively comfortable private room, with a ladder giving access to a bedroom above. The 'low end' of the house, reached by doors in the cross-wall opposite the dining table, could comprise either a single room that served in winter as a cattle shed (keeping the livestock safe from theft and providing warmth for the bedchamber above), or a combination of pantry and dairy. The three-part division of the house was also found, in essence, in manor houses and even in the palaces of kings and archbishops.

The garth behind the longhouse was small but productive. Peasants grew onions, leeks, garlic, brassicas, herbs, often fruit trees (pear, apple and sometimes cherry), as well as, in some cases, flax and hemp for making cloth and twine. The garth perhaps also contained a beehive. Against one of the walls lay the dunghill, onto which was thrown any domestic rubbish not given to the pig, to await scattering on the arable fields in autumn and spring.

A gate in the toft's rear boundary gave access to the croft – a long strip of enclosed land, which in the case of the West Row extended for about 100m, almost to the modern hedgeline. Within this, the family might keep cows, sheep, pigs, geese and, almost invariably, chickens.

## NORTH MANOR AND NORTH ROW

After 1254, the so-called North Manor was almost certainly home to several generations of the Percy family. Before then, it is uncertain whether it was occupied by the Percys or just part of the arable fields. It has barely been excavated, yet its form and development can be inferred from its well-preserved earthworks. Like the South Manor, it comprised a complex of buildings within a walled compound, but here the house was located centrally, affording greater privacy. A planned row of six tofts and crofts known as the North Row adjoined the

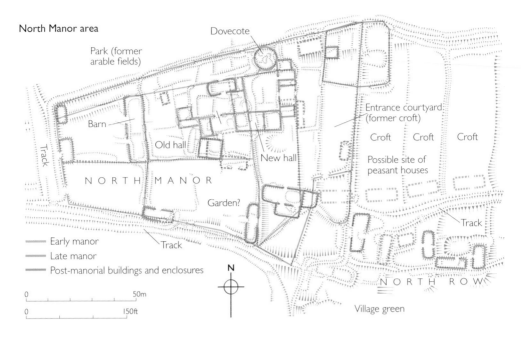

**North Manor area**

Park (former arable fields)

Dovecote

Barn

Old hall

New hall

Entrance courtyard (former croft)

Croft    Croft    Croft

Possible site of peasant houses

NORTH MANOR

Garden?

Track

Track

Track

Early manor
Late manor
Post-manorial buildings and enclosures

N

0          50m
0          150ft

NORTH ROW

Village green

east side of the manorial compound, forming a 'head row' across the end of the village green. It was presumably occupied by 'villein' families tied to the Percys.

The manor house, originally a fairly modest building, was greatly enlarged at some stage, with a new hall range and a new entrance courtyard on the site of what had been one of the peasant crofts. Either Peter Percy I or his son Robert III (c.1245–1321) may have instigated this redesign in the second half of the 13th century. Two buildings within the compound can be interpreted with confidence. To the west, a 28m-long building with two sets of opposing doorways must be the manorial threshing barn mentioned in a

document of 1368. The doorways nearest the manor house were blocked at some point, perhaps to convert the barn into a sheep house, reflecting the changing economy. Near the hedgeline to the north, a ring-shaped mound represents the foundations of a dovecote: a tall, circular building which would have overlooked the manor's entrance court. These elegant buildings were commonly linked to high-status residences in the Middle Ages, and provided eggs and birds for eating, feathers for stuffing pillows, and dung for fertilizing vegetable beds. Documents of the 1320s mention a park for hunting deer.

*Below: 14th-century illustration of noblemen hunting deer*

This may have appropriated part of the medieval open fields to the north. While entertainment may have been the park's primary function, it also offered a supply of meat, skins, and antlers for fine carving.

## ARABLE 'OPEN FIELDS'

Beyond and just within the hedges that presently surround the site lay the village's open fields: vast tracts of narrow, snaking 'rigs', or strip fields, arranged in large blocks unenclosed by hedges, fences or walls. The last of the open fields were converted to pasture in 1527. Today, only fragments of the distinctive ridges of these fields survive around the edges of the village. The rest were completely erased by modern ploughing which began in the 1950s.

The 'reverse-S' shape of each medieval rig was a result of the use of teams of up to eight oxen to draw the plough. The team swung off the straight ploughed line to give itself a wide space in which to turn at the end of the field. Teams of horses produced much straighter rigs, because they were more manoeuvrable. Although bones excavated at Wharram show that horses were used to draw ploughs from perhaps as early as the 13th century, the long-established curving pattern created by the oxen was carefully maintained until 1527.

Each 'villein' household nominally held one 'oxgang' or 'bovate' of land, covering about 7.3ha divided into about 15 rigs. Each rig would have been planted with barley, wheat, oats, peas or beans (in decreasing order of importance), or left fallow to be grazed (and manured) by up to three cows or horses, three pigs or 30 sheep. The produce from this land usually gave a peasant family a sufficient living, but not a comfortable one. From the 13th century onwards a land market developed in

*Above: An RAF aerial photograph of 1946 shows the ridges of the medieval open fields to the south-east of the village, which have now been largely ploughed flat*

England, allowing wealthier peasants to acquire more oxgangs. A valuation of 1323 shows that ten Percy tenants held 41 oxgangs between them, probably reflecting acquisitions in the wake of the Great Famine of 1315–17, when crops failed for three successive, exceptionally wet summers. Two or more oxgangs could generate a wider variety of produce and a decent surplus which could be sold to allow a higher standard of living.

*Below: Peasants ploughing with a team of four oxen from a manuscript illustration of about 1330*

# History of Wharram Percy

## EARLIEST SETTLEMENT

In the Late Iron Age, about 50 BC, a series of farm enclosures was established alongside the ancient east–west track that crosses the valley extending under the site of the North Manor. In the Roman period, about the third century AD, one of these compounds evolved into a larger enclosed farmstead, which survived well into the fifth century. It was once thought that this represented the seeds of village life at Wharram Percy, but the abandonment of the farmstead seems to have been followed by a period of almost complete desertion. By the sixth or seventh century, two small Anglo-Saxon buildings were built within the deeply worn trackway that had connected the earlier farmsteads to nearby settlements.

## MIDDLE SAXON SETTLEMENT: 650–850

Despite decades of research, how and when the village originated remains a topic of debate. Geophysical survey on the plateau in 2002 revealed several ditches, perhaps representing a cluster of oval enclosures, no traces of which survive on the surface. Excavations within these enclosures had recovered Middle Saxon material, and evidence of a few small buildings.

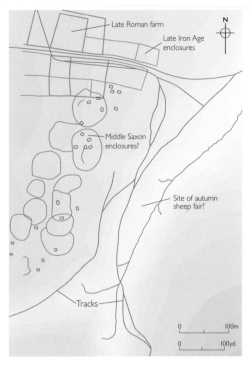

*Above: A plan of the settlement at Wharram in about 800*
*Below: Fragment of the arm of a Middle Saxon stone cross carved with a plait pattern, perhaps representing the Trinity*

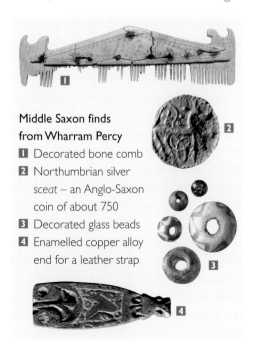

Middle Saxon finds from Wharram Percy

1. Decorated bone comb
2. Northumbrian silver *sceat* – an Anglo-Saxon coin of about 750
3. Decorated glass beads
4. Enamelled copper alloy end for a leather strap

From this, some scholars have inferred that a proto-village may have developed as early as the mid seventh century. Others argue that these small buildings were not permanent dwellings, but temporary huts erected by lowland sheep farmers who drove their flocks onto the open pastures of the Wolds to graze in summer and autumn. They suggest that the enclosures were sheepfolds connected with an annual market or fair held – as was often the case – around 11 November, the feast-day of St Martin (to whom the church was eventually dedicated). A fragment of a stone cross discovered in the excavations may have stood at the heart of the market place. Perhaps it was the location of an annual market at the junction of ancient long-distance routes, with access to a constant stream, that eventually led to the establishment of a permanent settlement here; a genuine village. This was not until the Late Saxon period.

## LATE SAXON OCCUPATION: 850–1066

At some point between 850 and 950 a major reorganization led to the establishment of the first basic components of the village, the remains of which can be seen today, including the first wooden church upon the green. This development must have been accompanied by a revolution in the wider landscape: the agreement of rights, of parish boundaries and of the extents of arable fields. Such transformations were widespread in the English countryside from the late ninth century onwards. The Middle Saxon enclosures and all traces of the small buildings that accompanied them were apparently ploughed flat before the new village was founded. This suggests a concerted effort, but whether this was directed by a landowner or by the community as a whole remains uncertain.

According to Domesday Book of 1086, the two main landowners in 'Warron' prior to the Norman Conquest were Lagmann and Carli, while a third man, Ketilbjorn, held a smaller portion of land. These men, whose names all betray Viking ancestry, were perhaps the most prominent of the village's many free peasants. They may have been among those responsible for rebuilding St Martin's church in stone shortly before the Conquest (see page 6). After Domesday, the surviving documents provide no further indication of the involvement of free peasants in village life: for this we must turn to the archaeological evidence.

### Late Saxon finds from Wharram Percy
These copper alloy fittings for a leather belt were made in Scandinavia

*Above: Mid 11th-century grave slabs were found to be the reused lids of Roman stone coffins*
*Below: The discovery of this Nine Men's Morris gameboard at Wharram reveals the lighter side of peasant life*

## RISE OF THE PERCY FAMILY: 1066–1254

In 1069–70 William the Conqueror carried out a devastating military campaign to subjugate northern England, known as the 'Harrying of the North'. As a result, by 1086 all the land in Wharram had been confiscated by the new Norman king. Lagmann and Carli's former holdings were granted to Osbert the Sheriff of York and Lincoln, while Ketilbjorn's was perhaps given at this time to William de Percy (d.c.1096), an important baron who had emigrated to England from Percy-en-Auge, Normandy, in 1067. William de Percy's descendants included some of the most famous knights of the medieval era: the Northumberland Percys, who built the great castles at Alnwick and Warkworth. The Percys who acquired the lordship of Wharram were a minor branch of this family, or perhaps even merely

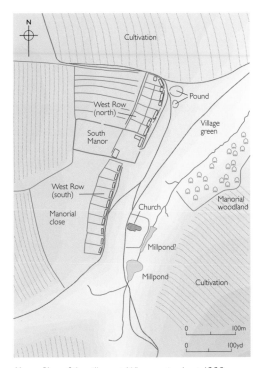

*Above:* Plan of the village at Wharram in about 1200

## THE VILLAGE'S GOLDEN ERA: 1254–1315

In 1254, Henry Chamberlain sold all his remaining rights in Wharram to Peter Percy I (c.1206–66), making the Percys all-powerful within the village. The name Wharram Percy probably entered common usage soon after, although it first appears in documents in 1292. It seems likely that soon after 1254 Peter Percy I demolished the South Manor, which may have been the Percys' property up to that point, or may have been owned by the Chamberlain family. It is not known whether the Percys already owned the North Manor, or whether they moved there from the South Manor. It is also possibly about this time that the North and East Rows were laid out, increasing the number of properties in the village to about 40, implying a population of perhaps about 200. Between 1261 and 1263, Peter I served as High Sheriff of Yorkshire. A valuation of 1267, made in the wake of his death, shows that the extent of the farmed land – the village's economic base – had remained fairly constant since Domesday.

Prosperity continued under the lordship of Peter I's son Robert Percy III (1245–1321), who may have been responsible for major changes to the North Manor (see page 13). Records made after his death mention a small hunting park (of about 3.25ha), a typical feature of a successful noble estate. With Robert III's twin sons, Henry and Peter II, respectively installed

descended from an important tenant who took on the surname of his overlord (though in later centuries the lesser family certainly claimed a blood relationship). Their main land holding was in Bolton Percy, but the remainder of their estates were scattered across Yorkshire.

By a marriage with Milicent, grand-daughter of Osbert the Sheriff, Herbert Chamberlain, a descendant of the Chamberlain of the King of Scotland, acquired the large land holding that had once belonged to Lagmann and Carli. But in about 1176, William Percy (d. between 1209 and 1213) acquired rights from the Montfort family over more land in Wharram, accruing a debt of 100 marks – the equivalent of about £160,000 today. This acquisition, together with the Percys' existing land holding, made them the major power in the village and obliged them to establish a permanent presence there. It is against this background that we should understand the building of the South Manor, the foundation of the adjacent well-ordered row of peasant tofts and crofts, and successive additions and changes to the church. It is still debated, however, whether these developments represent an assertion by the Chamberlains of their continuing interest, or by the Percys of their growing power.

*Below:* 13th-century nobles dining at a high table, so called because it stood on a raised platform or 'dais'

# Learning from Wharram's excavated human bones

Unprecedented excavations between 1962 and 1974 investigated the interior of St Martin's church and the northern half of the graveyard; the southern half, which retains gravestones bearing surnames still current in the local area, was left intact. The archaeologists recovered 687 skeletons. Scientific analyses of the bones have revealed fascinating details about everyday life in the village.

Children were generally breast-fed until they were about 18 months old; this was effective in providing good nutrition and immunity, for the infant mortality rate was about 15%, far lower than the 40% common in towns. As soon as breast-feeding ended, however, the child's problems began: rickets, a disease associated with severe malnutrition and lack of access to sunlight, was quite common in children under five. Since outdoor life must have been the norm for this farming community, these children may have had other illnesses that prevented them from going outside, as well as very poor diets. One ten-year-old boy died of leprosy.

A generally poor diet slowed children's growth, so that by the time they were 14, they were no taller than a modern ten year old, and even shorter than children of the same age living in

19th-century slums. It seems, however, that people continued to grow into their twenties, for adult males averaged 5ft 6in (1.68m), and females 5ft 2in (1.57m), only a little shorter than modern adults.

Bone fractures, arthritis and bone growth left by cuts and bangs all testify to the hardship of a farming life, while instances of tuberculosis point to unexpectedly frequent contact with nearby towns, where

infectious diseases were much more common. Despite these dangers, 40% of adults lived to be over 50 and some individuals with serious physical disabilities from birth were evidently cared for well enough to reach adulthood. A delicate trepanning operation (where a piece of the skull is removed) by an 11th-century surgeon certainly saved the life of a man bludgeoned over the head. Some treatment was less successful. When a 12th-century woman died of tuberculosis, a Caesarean operation may have been attempted to save the life of her unborn baby. It failed: the baby was buried between the mother's thighs.

*Above: Archaeologists excavating the interior of St Martin's Church in 1974*
*Left: A 13th-century manuscript illustration of a surgeon operating on a man's head. The patient holds a bowl to catch blood*

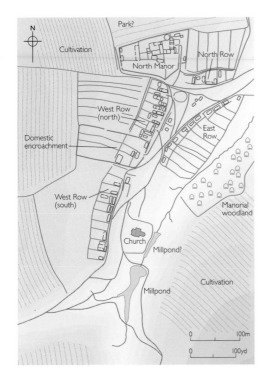

*Above: Plan of the village of Wharram Percy in about 1300*
*Below: Burial of plague victims in 1349 from a contemporary Belgian manuscript*

as the village's rector and lined up to take over the Wharram Percy manor, and his third son, Edmund, provided with a decent income from a manor at Stainborough, near Barnsley, the future must have seemed bright for the Percys, and for their village.

## A STEEP DECLINE: 1315–52

After a century of good fortune for the Percys, a series of tragedies struck in quick succession. In 1315, Robert III's son Peter II died aged about 25 without any male heir. This may have been an indirect consequence of the Great Famine that ravaged northern Europe from 1315 to 1317, resulting from successive crop failures. His death left his wife, Isabel, to care for their infant daughter Eustachia (c.1313–66), who may have had mental health problems from birth, and newborn baby Joan. In 1321, at the age of 76, Robert III died, followed a few years later by his son Henry.

Uncertainty about the succession of lordship would doubtless have been very troubling for the Percys' tenants, but more problems followed: Scots raids in 1322 – a consequence of Edward II's weak rule – also seem to have had an impact on the village's fortunes. A valuation of 1323 seems to show that there had been a severe economic downturn, with two-thirds of the village's land uncultivated, plots unoccupied and the village's two watermills disused. To restore stability, Eustachia was married as soon as possible, aged about 14, to Walter Heslerton (from the nearby village of that name). Four years later she gave birth to a son, also called Walter (1331–67). By 1334, although there were still at least 18 households, including the manor and the parsonage, Wharram Percy ranked 33rd of 50 local villages in a tax assessment. Its valuation of 18 shillings was not much more than half the average.

In 1349 the Black Death killed the elder Walter Heslerton. The younger Walter was still a minor and could not legally inherit the Wharram Percy estate. Royal officials successfully claimed that his mother, Eustachia,

## The Black Death

'Men and women carried the bodies of their own little ones to church on their shoulders and threw them into mass graves, from which arose such a stink that it was barely possible for anyone to go past a churchyard.' Chronicle of the Black Death, Rochester, 1314–50

*Above: Manuscript illustration of about 1330 showing a watermill with a fishing net and an eel trap in the millpond*

because of her mental condition (whether real or otherwise), should come under the protection of the king. This allowed the Crown to manipulate the management of her Wharram Percy estate for its own profit. Though the burial place of the plague victims remains undiscovered, it has been estimated that the village's population as a whole was reduced from about 67 to 45; this was severe enough to prompt a rebate of nearly one third in the tax collection of 1352.

## A PARTIAL RECOVERY: 1352–1450

In 1366, Eustachia died, but her 35-year-old son, Walter II, only outlived his mother by a year. On his death in 1367, the estate reverted to a distant relative, Henry, of the more

*Below: St Martin's Church, 1954. The arms of the Hilton family, in the form of two carved shields, can just be seen on the upper storey of the bell tower*
*Below right: The Hilton family arms from St Martin's Church*

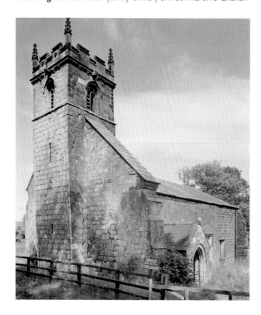

illustrious Percys of Spofforth Castle, ending the family's direct involvement in the village. A valuation made in the wake of Walter II's death shows that by 1368 although the buildings of the North Manor were still standing, they were in need of extensive repairs which made the property worth nothing in terms of taxation. Despite this, 30 houses within the village were occupied, all the arable land left uncultivated in 1323 was once more in use, one of the mills was working profitably, and both the millponds generated an income from fishing. In short, the households of the late 14th century, though fewer in number, were considerably better off, as shown by the excavated large peasant longhouse overlooking the church (see page 9). It is against this background that we must understand the fearsome Peasants' Revolt of 1381, triggered by the imposition of a harsh poll tax in 1377. The Revolt received widespread support in Yorkshire and Wharram's tax return suggests that much more than half the village's population had deliberately evaded paying.

At some point between 1394 and 1402, the Percy family of Spofforth exchanged the Wharram Percy manor for a manor at Shilbottle in Northumberland owned by the Hilton family of Hilton (now Hylton) Castle, near Sunderland. Baron William Hilton (1376–1435) immediately stamped his family's mark on Wharram's church but the family may never have resided at Wharram and certainly not after 1406. When William died in 1435 at least 16 houses were occupied.

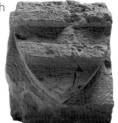

## 16TH-CENTURY ENCLOSURES AND THE END OF VILLAGE LIFE

Over the course of the late Middle Ages, the rising price of wool, the raw material for England's increasingly profitable export of woollen cloth, induced many landowners to switch to sheep farming, converting arable land to pasture. This sea-change spelled disaster for many small English communities which had lived by the plough for centuries. Yet at the same time, sheep pastures formed a protective carpet of turf over the remains of peasants' abandoned houses, streets and fields, allowing them to survive to the present as tell-tale mounds and hollows.

A witness statement refers to the eviction of four families and the deliberate destruction of their houses in Wharram at the instigation of William, 7th Baron Hilton (1451–1500) or his heir, the 8th Baron (d.1535), at some point between 1488 and 1506. Long thought to represent the final act of desertion, it is now seen as part of a longer process, for there seems to have been a sharp decrease in the village's population from 1458 onwards, perhaps caused by evictions that went unrecorded. It seems, too, that a few houses continued in occupation after 1500, probably as cottages for smallholders and shepherds, rather than as farmhouses. Baron Hilton finally abolished all the remaining arable strips in 1527, implying that a few peasant farmers may have continued to plough until that year when

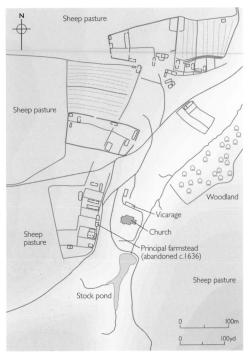

*Above: Plan of Wharram Percy in about 1500*

*Below: A peasant shears a sheep in an illustration of about 1500*

a decisive switch to sheep farming took place. In 1543–4 John Thorpe of Appleton kept 1,240 sheep under the care of just two shepherds on Wharram's former arable fields, which formed only part of his grazing lands. It may have been Thorpe who, in 1527, had offered Baron Hilton enough cash to evict the few remaining arable farmers. In lawsuits of 1555–6 relating to the rebuilding of the vicarage after fire damage,

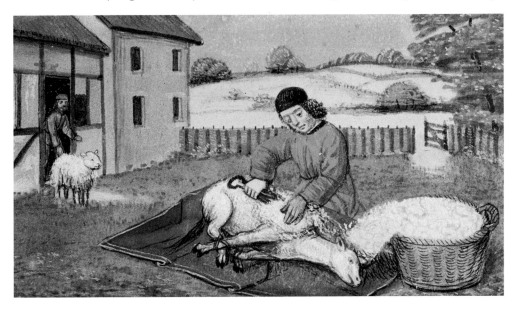

not one of the witnesses gave Wharram Percy as their place of residence. In 1573, Sir William Hilton sold the manor of Wharram Percy to Matthew Hutton (c.1529–1606), then Dean, and later Archbishop, of York.

By 1605 a 'chief messuage', or principal farmstead, is recorded, apparently operating a mixed agricultural regime, but with sheep farming playing the major role. This farmstead may equate to one of the best-preserved medieval longhouses, which as yet remains incompletely excavated (see page 9). Early 17th-century leases testify to the enclosure of former arable land with 'hedges and ditches sett with quickwood [hawthorn]'. Some of these were described as 'nowe decayed', suggesting that they might have been planted a century or more earlier. In 1634, Matthew Hutton's nephew, also called Matthew, sold the manor to Sir John Buck of Filey. Soon after 1636 the 'chief messuage' disappeared, marking the end of 700 years of continuous occupation.

# 'Inclosure': causes and effects

The famines and plagues of the earlier 14th century ushered in greater social mobility, coupled with mutual distrust between landlords and peasants. Many peasants regarded their traditional legal ties to a specific landlord and village as obsolete, and drifted into towns in search of prosperity. In their place, rural landlords often introduced sheep – placid tenants who offered a good income. Less scrupulous lords forcibly evicted tenants to free up land for grazing. The 'inclosure' of former open arable fields with stock-proof hedges and drystone walls became a powerful symbol of the new socio-economic reality. For peasants content with living on their land in villages that had been home since birth, eviction was a catastrophe. Sixteenth-century writers, with an emerging social conscience, described their fall: 'those miserable people… are all forced to change their seats, not knowing whither to go; and they must sell, almost for nothing, their household stuff. …When that little money is at an end (for it will be soon spent), what is left for them to do but either to steal, and so to be hanged … or to go about and beg?' Thomas More, *Utopia*, 1516.

*Above: Portrait of Thomas More (detail), by Hans Holbein, 1527*
*Below: 16th-century woodcut of a beggar being whipped through the streets of a town*

*Above: An etching of Matthew Hutton, Archbishop of York, copied from a contemporary portrait*

*Below: Detail from the first Ordnance Survey map showing the village earthworks as surveyed in 1850–51*

## POST-MEDIEVAL FARMS

By 1674, a farmhouse had been built and William Botterell was probably installed as its first tenant (see page 4). The adjacent farmyard was complete by about 1800 and a new farmhouse was built in 1807. Apart from a brief interlude during the Civil War when it was confiscated by the Parliamentarians, the land remained with the descendants of the Buck family until Henry Willoughby, 6th Baron Middleton (1761–1835), bought it in 1833. The names of the three fields that covered the site of the village at that date – Water Lane, Towngate and Town Street – betray a continued folk memory of the village. Less than 15 years later, Henry Lord Middleton's heir, Digby Willoughby, 7th Baron Middleton (1769–1856), demolished the farmhouse and most of the late 18th-century farmyard, but converted one range into the row of cottages initially called Low House, which had become known as Wharram Percy Cottages by 1888.

## REDISCOVERY, EXCAVATION AND PRESENTATION

Before the 1950s, medieval settlements attracted little academic study. Scholars mainly focused on the administrative organization of the countryside – how the feudal system operated through manors and estates. Although Wharram's earthworks had been accurately mapped by the Ordnance Survey in

1850–51 and labelled as the site of a lost village, by the early decades of the 20th century academics were questioning how widespread such deserted settlements had been. The economic historian Maurice Beresford (1920–2005) began mapping tracts of strip fields in the Midlands to prove that medieval rural desertion was a real and widespread phenomenon. On 17 June 1948, researchers interested in the topic held a meeting at Cambridge University. This prompted Beresford's first visit to Wharram Percy nine days later, as he was intrigued by the isolated church shown on the then-current Ordnance Survey map. A month later, aerial photographer J K St Joseph (1912–94), one of the other participants in the 17 June meeting, took some of the best aerial photographs of the site.

Beresford was most familiar with Midlands villages where the sites of medieval houses are difficult to identify because they were built using organic materials. At Wharram, he was immediately impressed by the crisp wall-lines left by stone foundations, which were also clear at ground level. Following a broadcast on local radio, Beresford was invited to excavate at Wharram, which he began to do in the summer of 1950, assisted by a small group of his own students and a few local enthusiasts. These initial efforts were, by his own admission, 'primitive' and when archaeologist John Hurst (1927–2003) joined Beresford in 1952, he was reportedly quietly horrified. The two men's different skills and interests complemented each other, however, and their 50-year partnership at Wharram led to profound shifts in archaeological theory and practice, as well as

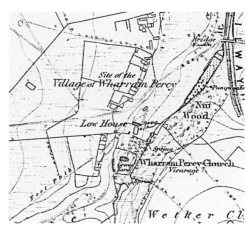

to several highly influential books. Excavations took place every summer until 1990. They were at the cutting edge of research and became a test-bed for new techniques and a training ground for many young archaeologists.

When Beresford first visited in 1948, the Milner family were still living in Wharram Percy Cottages. When the cottages were finally vacated in 1976, they became a hostel for the diggers. Although the archaeological site has been in the care of English Heritage since 1974, all the land that comprised the medieval manor, which in turn probably corresponds to that held by Lagmann, Carli and Ketilbjorn, is still owned by Lord Middleton of Birdsall.

*Above:* Beresford, Hurst, students and the Milner family outside Wharram Percy Cottages in the 1950s

# Pioneering archaeology at Wharram

The history of cutting-edge research at Wharram began with economic historian Maurice Beresford's unprecedented desire to understand the everyday lives of ordinary medieval people. He welcomed new ideas brought by other experts. In 1948, J K St Joseph, a geologist turned aerial photographer, convinced him of the worth of that technique, while Danish archaeologist Axel Steensberg (1906–99) introduced the concept of excavating large areas, rather than dozens of small trenches on a grid. 'Open area excavation' – the norm today – was first put into practice at Wharram in 1953, after Beresford's meeting with pottery specialist John Hurst, who was to become co-director of the project. This new method allowed them to understand relationships

between archaeological layers in plan as they progressed, rather than in hindsight from vertical 'sections'. Beresford and Hurst's desire to pass knowledge on to others resulted in arguably the project's greatest legacy: the large number of archaeologists who owe their careers to training received at Wharram.

*Right: Maurice Beresford (left) and John Hurst (right) in St Martin's church in the 1980s*